T0375295

Cursive Writing Workbook

Casaundra Davis

authorHOUSE

AuthorHouse™
1663 Liberty Drive
Bloomington, IN 47403
www.authorhouse.com
Phone: 833-262-8899

© 2024 Casaundra Davis. All rights reserved.

No part of this book may be reproduced, stored in a retrieval system, or transmitted by any means without the written permission of the author.

Published by AuthorHouse 05/30/2024

ISBN: 979-8-8230-2754-0 (sc)
ISBN: 979-8-8230-2751-9 (e)

Print information available on the last page.

Any people depicted in stock imagery provided by Getty Images are models, and such images are being used for illustrative purposes only.
Certain stock imagery © Getty Images.

This book is printed on acid-free paper.

Because of the dynamic nature of the Internet, any web addresses or links contained in this book may have changed since publication and may no longer be valid. The views expressed in this work are solely those of the author and do not necessarily reflect the views of the publisher, and the publisher hereby disclaims any responsibility for them.

Learning is the Key To Success

Support children learning with this engaging activity workbook !

Workbooks I designed is to help reinforce important skills learned in the classroom. To help the subject fun and challenging-

The workbook was designed and created By: I So Crafty Creations

UPERCASE LETTERS

trace and repeat

UPERCASE LETTERS

trace and repeat

$\mathcal{B}$ $\mathcal{B}$ $\mathcal{B}$ $\mathcal{B}$ $\mathcal{B}$

$\mathcal{B}$ $\mathcal{B}$ $\mathcal{B}$ $\mathcal{B}$ $\mathcal{B}$

$\mathcal{B}$ $\mathcal{B}$ $\mathcal{B}$ $\mathcal{B}$ $\mathcal{B}$

$\mathcal{B}$ $\mathcal{B}$ $\mathcal{B}$ $\mathcal{B}$ $\mathcal{B}$

$\mathcal{B}$ $\mathcal{B}$ $\mathcal{B}$ $\mathcal{B}$ $\mathcal{B}$

UPERCASE LETTERS

trace and repeat

$\mathcal{C}$ $\mathcal{C}$ $\mathcal{C}$ $\mathcal{C}$ $\mathcal{C}$

$\mathcal{C}$ $\mathcal{C}$ $\mathcal{C}$ $\mathcal{C}$ $\mathcal{C}$

$\mathcal{C}$ $\mathcal{C}$ $\mathcal{C}$ $\mathcal{C}$ $\mathcal{C}$

$\mathcal{C}$ $\mathcal{C}$ $\mathcal{C}$ $\mathcal{C}$ $\mathcal{C}$

$\mathcal{C}$ $\mathcal{C}$ $\mathcal{C}$ $\mathcal{C}$ $\mathcal{C}$

UPERCASE LETTERS

trace and repeat

$\mathcal{D}$ $\mathcal{D}$ $\mathcal{D}$ $\mathcal{D}$ $\mathcal{D}$

$\mathcal{D}$ $\mathcal{D}$ $\mathcal{D}$ $\mathcal{D}$ $\mathcal{D}$

$\mathcal{D}$ $\mathcal{D}$ $\mathcal{D}$ $\mathcal{D}$ $\mathcal{D}$

$\mathcal{D}$ $\mathcal{D}$ $\mathcal{D}$ $\mathcal{D}$ $\mathcal{D}$

$\mathcal{D}$ $\mathcal{D}$ $\mathcal{D}$ $\mathcal{D}$ $\mathcal{D}$

UPERCASE LETTERS

trace and repeat

$\mathcal{E}$ $\mathcal{E}$ $\mathcal{E}$ $\mathcal{E}$ $\mathcal{E}$

$\mathcal{E}$ $\mathcal{E}$ $\mathcal{E}$ $\mathcal{E}$ $\mathcal{E}$

$\mathcal{E}$ $\mathcal{E}$ $\mathcal{E}$ $\mathcal{E}$ $\mathcal{E}$

$\mathcal{E}$ $\mathcal{E}$ $\mathcal{E}$ $\mathcal{E}$ $\mathcal{E}$

$\mathcal{E}$ $\mathcal{E}$ $\mathcal{E}$ $\mathcal{E}$ $\mathcal{E}$

UPERCASE LETTERS

trace and repeat

$\mathcal{F}$ $\mathcal{F}$ $\mathcal{F}$ $\mathcal{F}$ $\mathcal{F}$

$\mathcal{F}$ $\mathcal{F}$ $\mathcal{F}$ $\mathcal{F}$ $\mathcal{F}$

$\mathcal{F}$ $\mathcal{F}$ $\mathcal{F}$ $\mathcal{F}$ $\mathcal{F}$

$\mathcal{F}$ $\mathcal{F}$ $\mathcal{F}$ $\mathcal{F}$ $\mathcal{F}$

$\mathcal{F}$ $\mathcal{F}$ $\mathcal{F}$ $\mathcal{F}$ $\mathcal{F}$

UPERCASE LETTERS
trace and repeat

G G G G G

G G G G G

G G G G G

G G G G G

G G G G G

UPERCASE LETTERS

trace and repeat

$\mathcal{H}$ $\mathcal{H}$ $\mathcal{H}$ $\mathcal{H}$ $\mathcal{H}$

$\mathcal{H}$ $\mathcal{H}$ $\mathcal{H}$ $\mathcal{H}$ $\mathcal{H}$

$\mathcal{H}$ $\mathcal{H}$ $\mathcal{H}$ $\mathcal{H}$ $\mathcal{H}$

$\mathcal{H}$ $\mathcal{H}$ $\mathcal{H}$ $\mathcal{H}$ $\mathcal{H}$

$\mathcal{H}$ $\mathcal{H}$ $\mathcal{H}$ $\mathcal{H}$ $\mathcal{H}$

UPERCASE LETTERS
trace and repeat

UPERCASE LETTERS

trace and repeat

UPERCASE LETTERS

trace and repeat

UPERCASE LETTERS

trace and repeat

UPERCASE LETTERS

trace and repeat

$\mathcal{M}$ $\mathcal{M}$ $\mathcal{M}$ $\mathcal{M}$ $\mathcal{M}$

$\mathcal{M}$ $\mathcal{M}$ $\mathcal{M}$ $\mathcal{M}$ $\mathcal{M}$

$\mathcal{M}$ $\mathcal{M}$ $\mathcal{M}$ $\mathcal{M}$ $\mathcal{M}$

$\mathcal{M}$ $\mathcal{M}$ $\mathcal{M}$ $\mathcal{M}$ $\mathcal{M}$

$\mathcal{M}$ $\mathcal{M}$ $\mathcal{M}$ $\mathcal{M}$ $\mathcal{M}$

UPERCASE LETTERS

trace and repeat

UPERCASE LETTERS

trace and repeat

UPERCASE LETTERS

trace and repeat

UPERCASE LETTERS

trace and repeat

Q Q Q Q Q

Q Q Q Q Q

Q Q Q Q Q

Q Q Q Q Q

Q Q Q Q Q

UPERCASE LETTERS

trace and repeat

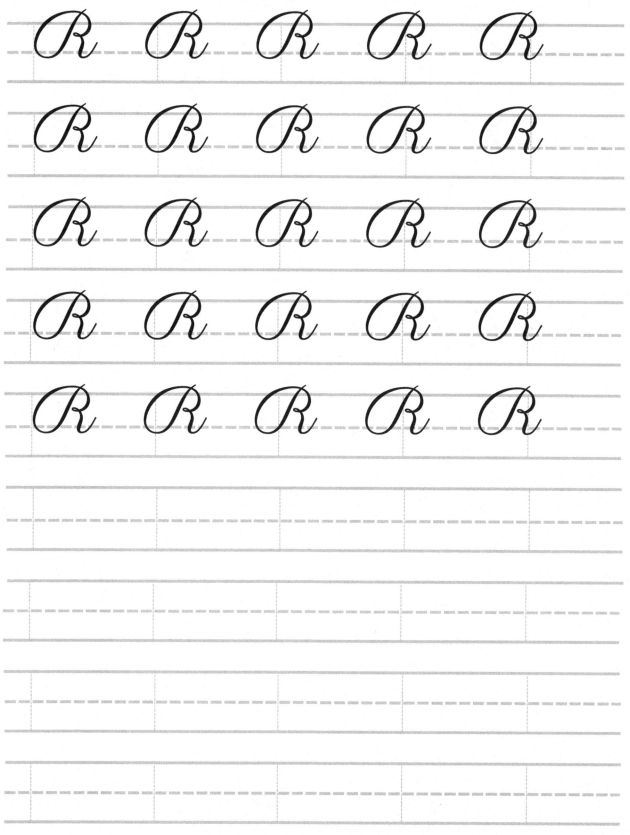

UPERCASE LETTERS

trace and repeat

UPERCASE LETTERS

trace and repeat

$\mathcal{F}$ $\mathcal{F}$ $\mathcal{F}$ $\mathcal{F}$ $\mathcal{F}$

$\mathcal{F}$ $\mathcal{F}$ $\mathcal{F}$ $\mathcal{F}$ $\mathcal{F}$

$\mathcal{F}$ $\mathcal{F}$ $\mathcal{F}$ $\mathcal{F}$ $\mathcal{F}$

$\mathcal{F}$ $\mathcal{F}$ $\mathcal{F}$ $\mathcal{F}$ $\mathcal{F}$

$\mathcal{F}$ $\mathcal{F}$ $\mathcal{F}$ $\mathcal{F}$ $\mathcal{F}$

UPERCASE LETTERS

trace and repeat

$\mathcal{U}$ $\mathcal{U}$ $\mathcal{U}$ $\mathcal{U}$ $\mathcal{U}$ $\mathcal{U}$

$\mathcal{U}$ $\mathcal{U}$ $\mathcal{U}$ $\mathcal{U}$ $\mathcal{U}$ $\mathcal{U}$

$\mathcal{U}$ $\mathcal{U}$ $\mathcal{U}$ $\mathcal{U}$ $\mathcal{U}$ $\mathcal{U}$

$\mathcal{U}$ $\mathcal{U}$ $\mathcal{U}$ $\mathcal{U}$ $\mathcal{U}$ $\mathcal{U}$

$\mathcal{U}$ $\mathcal{U}$ $\mathcal{U}$ $\mathcal{U}$ $\mathcal{U}$ $\mathcal{U}$

UPERCASE LETTERS

trace and repeat

$\mathcal{V}$ $\mathcal{V}$ $\mathcal{V}$ $\mathcal{V}$ $\mathcal{V}$

$\mathcal{V}$ $\mathcal{V}$ $\mathcal{V}$ $\mathcal{V}$ $\mathcal{V}$

$\mathcal{V}$ $\mathcal{V}$ $\mathcal{V}$ $\mathcal{V}$ $\mathcal{V}$

$\mathcal{V}$ $\mathcal{V}$ $\mathcal{V}$ $\mathcal{V}$ $\mathcal{V}$

$\mathcal{V}$ $\mathcal{V}$ $\mathcal{V}$ $\mathcal{V}$ $\mathcal{V}$

UPERCASE LETTERS

trace and repeat

$\mathcal{W}$ $\mathcal{W}$ $\mathcal{W}$ $\mathcal{W}$ $\mathcal{W}$

$\mathcal{W}$ $\mathcal{W}$ $\mathcal{W}$ $\mathcal{W}$ $\mathcal{W}$

$\mathcal{W}$ $\mathcal{W}$ $\mathcal{W}$ $\mathcal{W}$ $\mathcal{W}$

$\mathcal{W}$ $\mathcal{W}$ $\mathcal{W}$ $\mathcal{W}$ $\mathcal{W}$

$\mathcal{W}$ $\mathcal{W}$ $\mathcal{W}$ $\mathcal{W}$ $\mathcal{W}$

UPERCASE LETTERS

trace and repeat

$\mathcal{X}$ $\mathcal{X}$ $\mathcal{X}$ $\mathcal{X}$ $\mathcal{X}$

$\mathcal{X}$ $\mathcal{X}$ $\mathcal{X}$ $\mathcal{X}$ $\mathcal{X}$

$\mathcal{X}$ $\mathcal{X}$ $\mathcal{X}$ $\mathcal{X}$ $\mathcal{X}$

$\mathcal{X}$ $\mathcal{X}$ $\mathcal{X}$ $\mathcal{X}$ $\mathcal{X}$

$\mathcal{X}$ $\mathcal{X}$ $\mathcal{X}$ $\mathcal{X}$ $\mathcal{X}$

UPERCASE LETTERS

trace and repeat

Y Y Y Y Y

Y Y Y Y Y

Y Y Y Y Y

Y Y Y Y Y

Y Y Y Y Y

UPERCASE LETTERS

trace and repeat

lowercase letters

trace and repeat

a a a a a

a a a a a

a a a a a

a a a a a

a a a a a

lowercase letters

trace and repeat

b b b b b

b b b b b

b b b b b

b b b b b

b b b b b

lowercase letters

trace and repeat

C C C C C

C C C C C

C C C C C

C C C C C

C C C C C

lowercase letters
trace and repeat

d d d d d

d d d d d

d d d d d

d d d d d

d d d d d

lowercase letters
trace and repeat

e *e* *e* *e* *e*

e *e* *e* *e* *e*

e *e* *e* *e* *e*

e *e* *e* *e* *e*

e *e* *e* *e* *e*

lowercase letters
trace and repeat

f f f f f

f f f f f

f f f f f

f f f f f

f f f f f

lowercase letters
trace and repeat

g g g g g

g g g g g

g g g g g

g g g g g

g g g g g

lowercase letters
trace and repeat

h h h h h

h h h h h

h h h h h

h h h h h

h h h h h

lowercase letters
trace and repeat

i i i i i

i i i i i

i i i i i

i i i i i

i i i i i

lowercase letters

j   *j*   *j*   *j*   *j*

j   *j*   *j*   *j*   *j*

j   *j*   *j*   *j*   *j*

j   *j*   *j*   *j*   *j*

j   *j*   *j*   *j*   *j*

lowercase letters
trace and repeat

k k k k k

k k k k k

k k k k k

k k k k k

k k k k k

lowercase letters
trace and repeat

ℓ   ℓ   ℓ   ℓ   ℓ

ℓ   ℓ   ℓ   ℓ   ℓ

ℓ   ℓ   ℓ   ℓ   ℓ

ℓ   ℓ   ℓ   ℓ   ℓ

ℓ   ℓ   ℓ   ℓ   ℓ

lowercase letters
trace and repeat

m m m m m

m m m m m

m m m m m

m m m m m

m m m m m

lowercase letters
trace and repeat

n　　n　　n　　n　　n

n　　n　　n　　n　　n

n　　n　　n　　n　　n

n　　n　　n　　n　　n

n　　n　　n　　n　　n

lowercase letters
trace and repeat

O O O O O

O O O O O

O O O O O

O O O O O

O O O O O

lowercase letters
trace and repeat

p   *p*   *p*   *p*   *p*

p   *p*   *p*   *p*   *p*

p   *p*   *p*   *p*   *p*

p   *p*   *p*   *p*   *p*

p   *p*   *p*   *p*   *p*

lowercase letters

trace and
repeat

q   q   q   q   q

q   q   q   q   q

q   q   q   q   q

q   q   q   q   q

q   q   q   q   q

lowercase letters
trace and repeat

v v v v v

v v v v v

v v v v v

v v v v v

v v v v v

lowercase letters
trace and repeat

lowercase letters

trace and

repeat

u u u u u

u u u u u

u u u u u

u u u u u

u u u u u

lowercase letters
trace and repeat

t   *t*   *t*   *t*   *t*

t   *t*   *t*   *t*   *t*

t   *t*   *t*   *t*   *t*

t   *t*   *t*   *t*   *t*

t   *t*   *t*   *t*   *t*

lowercase letters

trace and repeat

lowercase letters
trace and repeat

w w w w w

w w w w w

w w w w w

w w w w w

w w w w w

lowercase letters
trace and repeat

x x x x x

x x x x x

x x x x x

x x x x x

x x x x x

lowercase letters

trace and
repeat

y y y y y

y y y y y

y y y y y

y y y y y

y y y y y

lowercase letters

trace and
repeat

Names of the Fruits

trace the letter

Apple   Apple

Banana   Banana

Orange   Orange

Grape   Grape

Mango   Mango

Plum   Plum

Kiwi   Kiwi

Pear   Pear

Peach   Peach

Names of the Fruits

repeat the fruit names

Names of the Vegetables

trace the letter

Carrot   Carrot

Pumpkin   Pumpkin

Onion   Onion

Spinach   Spinach

Turnip   Turnip

Potato   Potato

Beat   Beat

Cabbage   Cabbage

Beans   Beans

Names of the Vegetables

repeat the vegetables name

Names of the Colors

trace the letter

Red   Red

Yellow   Yellow

Orange   Orange

Pink   Pink

Blue   Blue

Purple   Purple

Black   Black

Green   Green

Peach   Peach

Names of the Colors

repeat the colors names

Names of the Animals

trace the letters

Dog Dog

Lion Lion

Kangaroo Kangaroo

Ostrich Ostrich

Duck Duck

Owl Owl

Panda Panda

Horse Horse

Elephant Elephant

Names of the Animals

repeat the animal names

Names of the Shapes

trace the letter

Square   Square

Triangle   Triangle

Oval   Oval

Rectangle   Rectangle

Star   Star

Hexagon   Hexagon

Octagon   Octagon

Pentagon   Pentagon

Circle   Circle

Names of the Shapes

repeat the shapes names

Names of the DAYS

trace the letter

Sunday Sunday

Monday Monday

Tuesday Tuesday

Wednesday Wednesday

Thursday Thursday

Friday Friday

Saturday Saturday

Names of the DAYS

repeat the days names

Names of the Body parts

trace the letterS

Head	Head
Eyes	Eyes
Mouth	Mouth
Shoulder	Shoulder
Chest	Chest
Elbow	Elbow
Hand	Hand
Finger	Finger
Knee	Knee

Names of the Body parts

repeat the body parts names

Names of the Months

trace the letter

January July

February August

March September

April October

May November

June December

January February March

April May June July

August September October

November December

Names of the Months

repeat the month names

Numbers

trace the letter

One   One

Two   Two

Three   Three

Four   Four

Five   Five

Six   Six

Seven   Seven

Eight   Eight

Nine   Nine

Numbers

repeat the numbers

Numbers

trace the numbers

1   1   1   1

2   2   2   2

3   3   3   3

4   4   4   4

5   5   5   5

6   6   6   6

7   7   7   7

8   8   8   8

9   9   9   9

Numbers

repeat the numbers

Cursive Letter writing practice

trace and repeat

The fat cat sat on a mat.

The rat ran to the van.

I see a big boat.

He looked at the price tag.

I see a flag.

Cursive Letter writing practice

trace and repeat

I see a red jet.

My pet hen is wet.

I see a web on the net.

Ted went to bed.

The man has a hat.

Cursive Letter writing practice

trace and repeat

You did a wonderful job.

Ava likes to play piano.

There is a bird in the tree.

What are you doing here.

Peter has a blue hat.

Cursive Letter writing pratice
trace and repeat

I can see the bus.

The farmers grow our food.

What is your name.

She has a pet dog.

I can run fast.

Cursive Letter writing practice

trace and repeat

A parrot can talk.

I like my red bike.

The water is hot.

Take the trash out.

I have a pet fish.

Cursive Letter writing practice

trace and repeat

She has a chicken.

It had many colors.

Do you see the rainbow.

The dog was barking.

My new shoes are white

Cursive Letter writing practice

trace and repeat

Tom has a bib.

Mom has a bag.

That bird is loud.

You are my best friend.

I have to go home.

Cursive Letter writing practice
trace and repeat

His top is wet.

The rug is red.

The pot has a lid.

Her lips are red

Kim has a bot.

Cursive Letter writing practice

trace and repeat

The bug is on the mug.

She will eat the nut.

This is my jug.

I like to cut.

They are on the bus.

Cursive Letter writing practice

trace and repeat

We went into the hut.

My cap is red.

She gave her a big hug.

The boy is sick in bed.

Bob has a pet frog.

Cursive Letter writing practice

trace and repeat

She is my mom.

The fan is off.

I like to eat apples.

The mug is pink.

I see the cats and dogs.

Cursive Letter writing practice

trace and repeat

She is my mom.

The fan is off.

I like to eat apples.

The bin is in the pit.

She put the dress on.

Shapes and Strokes practice

trace and repeat

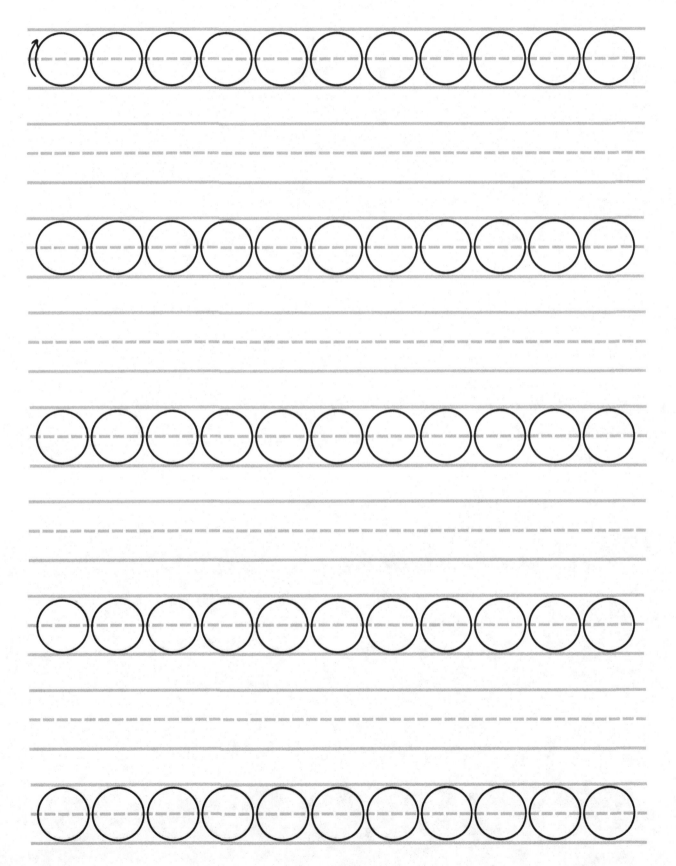

Shapes and Strokes practices

trace and repeat

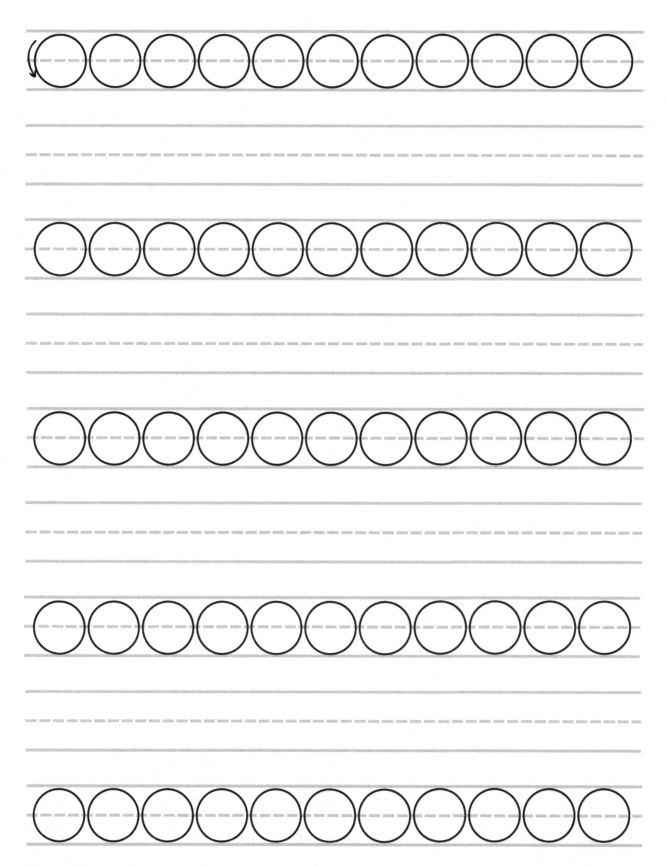

Shapes and Strokes practice

trace and repeat

Shapes and Strokes practice

trace and repeat

Shapes and Strokes practice

trace and repeat

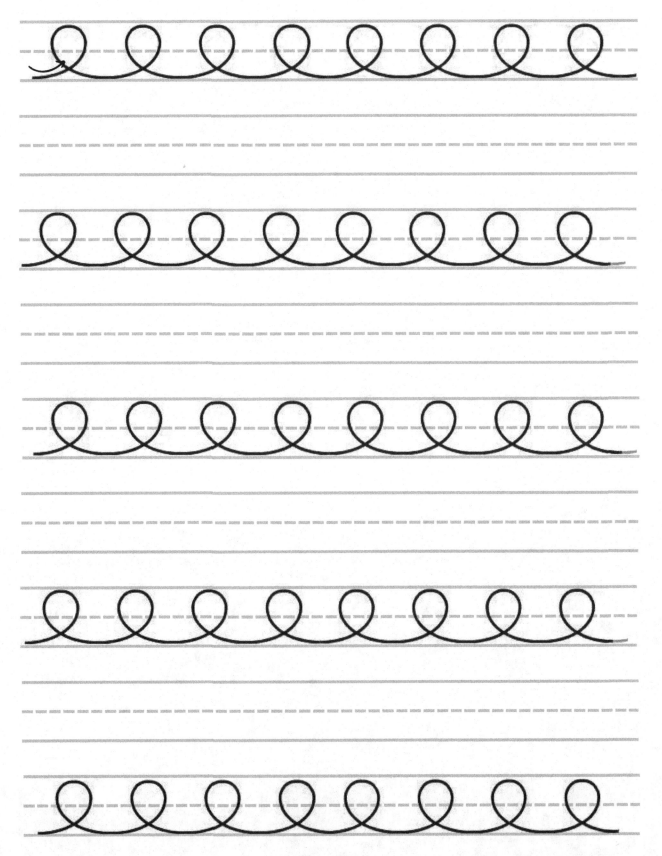

Shapes and Strokes practice

trace and repeat

Shapes and Strokes practice

trace and repeat

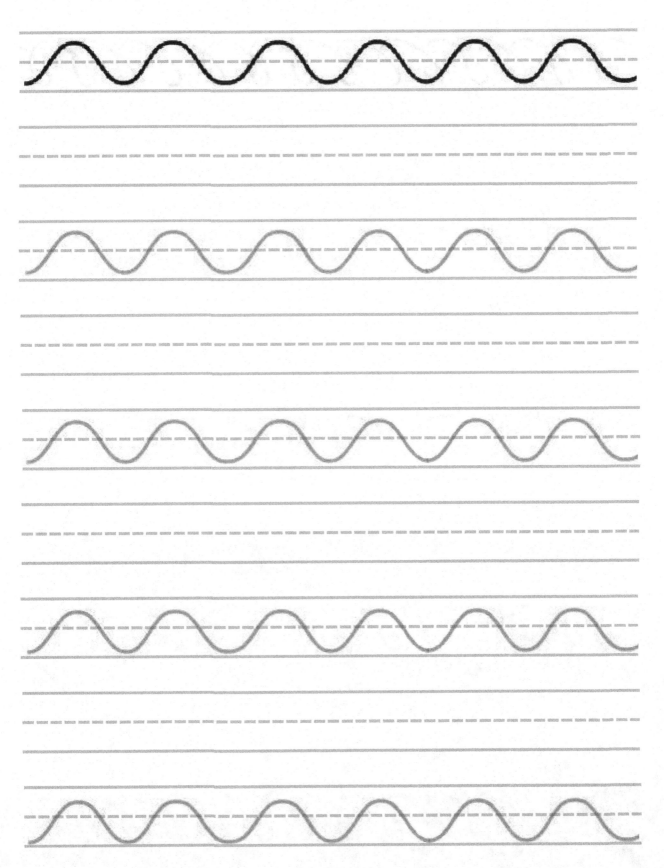

Shapes and Strokes practice

trace and repeat

Shapes and Strokes practice
trace and repeat

Shapes and Strokes practice

trace and repeat

94

Shapes and Strokes practice

trace and repeat

Shapes and Strokes practice
trace and repeat

Shapes and Strokes practice

trace and repeat

Shapes and Strokes practice

trace and repeat

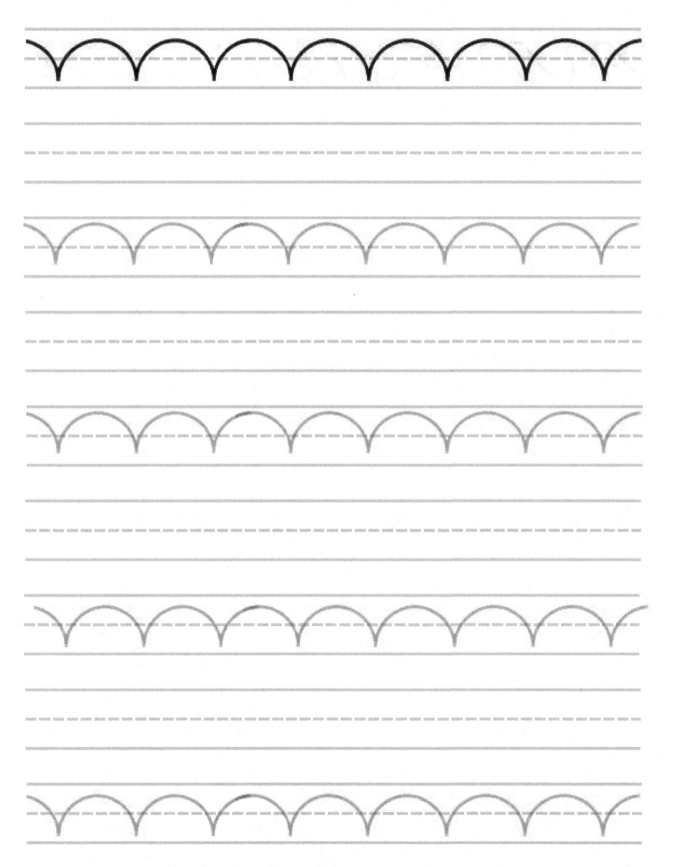

Shapes and Strokes practice

trace and repeat

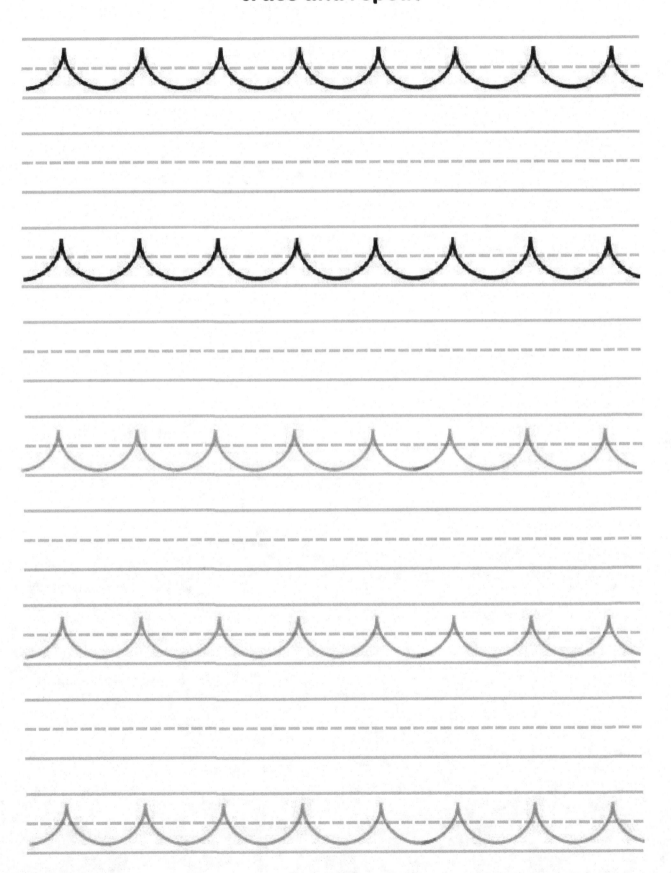

103